# The Last Days OF JESUS

## PARTICIPANT'S GUIDE

## The Deeper Connections Series

*The Miracles of Jesus*

*The Last Days of Jesus*

*The Forgiveness of Jesus*

*The Life of Jesus*

*The Parables of Jesus*

*The Prayers of Jesus*

# Deeper CONNECTIONS

# THE Last Days OF JESUS
## PARTICIPANT'S GUIDE

*Six In-depth Studies Connecting the Bible to Life*

## Matt Williams
### General Editor

ROSE
PUBLISHING

**Deeper Connections: The Last Days of Jesus Participant's Guide**

© 2009, 2016 by Matt Williams

Published by Rose Publishing
An imprint of Hendrickson Publishing Group
Rose Publishing, LLC
P.O. Box 3473
Peabody, Massachusetts 01961-3473
www.hendricksonpublishinggroup.com

ISBN 978-1-62862-433-5

*Cover Design: Jeff Gifford*
*Cover Photo: Masterfile*
*Interior Design: Mark Sheeres*

Printed in the United States of America
May 2020, 5th printing

# Contents

*Preface*. . . . . . . . . . . . . . . . . . . . . . . . . . *7*

*About the Video Teachers* . . . . . . . . . . . . . . . . . . . . . . *9*

*Session 1*    From Warrior to Servant . . . . . . . . . . . . . . . . . . 11
Jesus the Messiah (Matthew 16:13–28)
Dr. Matt Williams

*Session 2*    A Glimpse of Glory. . . . . . . . . . . . . . . . . . . . . . 33
The Transfiguration (Matthew 17:1–9)
Prof. Susan Hecht

*Session 3*    The Rejected King . . . . . . . . . . . . . . . . . . . . 53
The Triumphal Entry (Matthew 21:1–22)
Dr. Mark Strauss

*Session 4*    Love to the Full . . . . . . . . . . . . . . . . . . . . . 69
The Last Supper (John 13:1–5;
Matthew 26:21–29)
Dr. Scott Duvall

*Session 5*    The Ultimate Victory. . . . . . . . . . . . . . . . . . . 87
The Trial and Death of Jesus
(Luke 22:66–23:3; 23:32–34, 44–47)
Dr. Darrell Bock

*Session 6*    The Death of Death . . . . . . . . . . . . . . . . . . . . .107
The Resurrection of Jesus (Matthew 28:1–10)
Dr. Gary Burge

*Source Acknowledgments* . . . . . . . . . . . . . . . . . . . . . . . . . .*129*
*Map and Photo Credits* . . . . . . . . . . . . . . . . . . . . . . . . .*132*
*Books for Further Reading* . . . . . . . . . . . . . . . . . . . . . . . . .*133*

# *Preface*

We all know Christians who are bored with Bible study — not because the Bible is boring, but because they haven't been introduced to its meaning in its first-century context and how that is signifi cant for our lives today. When we begin to understand some of these "deeper connections" — both to the first century and to the twenty-first century — our lives are transformed.

The idea for the Deeper Connections series grew out of a concern that far too many Bible studies lack depth and solid biblical application. We wanted a Bible study series that was written and taught by biblical experts who could also communicate that material in a *clear, practical, understandable* manner. The Deeper Connections teachers have one foot in the historical, biblical text and the other in the modern world; they not only have written numerous books, they have many years of pastoral experience. When they teach in the local church, they often hear comments such as, "Wow, I've never heard it explained that way before." Unfortunately, that's because, until recently, Bible professors usually spent most of their time writing books for other professors, or occasionally for pastors, and the layperson in the church had little access to this biblical knowledge. Deeper Connections seeks to remedy this by bringing the best in biblical scholarship directly to small groups and Sunday school classes through the popular medium of DVD.

Don't be scared by the word "deeper" — deeper does not mean that these studies are hard to understand. It simply means that we are attempting to get at the true meaning of the biblical text, which involves investigating the historical, religious, and social background of first-century Jewish culture and their Greek and Roman neighbors. If we fail to study and understand this background, then we also fail to understand the deeper and true meaning of the Bible.

After making deeper connections to the biblical texts, the teachers then apply that text to life in the twenty-first century. This is where a deeper look into the text really pays off. Life-application in the church today has sometimes been a bit shallow and many times unrelated to the biblical passage itself. In this series, the practical application derives directly out of the biblical text.

So, to borrow the alternate title of *The Hobbit*, J. R. R. Tolkien's bestselling classic, we invite you to join us on an adventure to "there and back again"! Your life won't be the same as a result.

# *About the Video Teachers*

**Dr. Darrell Bock** is research professor of New Testament Studies at Dallas Theological Seminary in Dallas, Texas. An editor-at-large for *Christianity Today*, he speaks and teaches on the person of Jesus both nationally and internationally. Darrell is the author of more than twenty books, including a *New York Times* nonfiction bestseller and two commentaries on the gospel of Luke.

**Dr. Gary Burge** is professor of New Testament at Wheaton College in Wheaton, Illinois, and a sought-after conference speaker. His experiences in Beirut, Lebanon, in the early 1970s when civil war broke out have helped him to see how valuable it is to understand the world of the Middle East in order to correctly understand the biblical world of Jesus. Gary is the author of many books, including a commentary on the gospel of John.

**Dr. Scott Duvall** is professor of New Testament at Ouachita Baptist University in Little Rock, Arkansas, where he has won the Outstanding Faculty Award four times. He has pastored various churches, and presently is co-pastor of Fellowship Church in Arkadelphia, Arkansas. Scott has written many books on how to interpret, preach, and apply the Bible.

**Prof. Susan Hecht** is instructor of New Testament at Denver Seminary in Denver, Colorado. She is currently completing a doctorate in New Testament from Trinity Evangelical Divinity School, before which she ministered on college campuses with Campus Crusade for Christ for twenty years in Colorado, Oregon, and North Carolina. Susan has written on the topic of ministry to postmoderns.

**Dr. Mark Strauss** is professor of New Testament at Bethel Seminary in San Diego, California. He is a frequent preacher at San Diego area churches and has served in three interim pastorates. Mark is the author of many books, including a commentary on the gospel of Luke and *Four Portraits, One Jesus: An Introduction to Jesus and the Gospels.*

**Dr. Matt Williams** is associate professor of New Testament at Talbot School of Theology, Biola University, La Mirada, California. A former missionary to Spain, Matt preaches and teaches in churches throughout the United States and Spain. He is general editor of *Biblioteca Teológica Vida*, *Colección Teológica Contemporánea*, and *What the New Testament Authors Really Cared About*, and is the author of two books on the Gospels.

Host **Margaret Feinberg** (www.margaretfeinberg.com) is a popular speaker at churches and leading conferences such as Fusion, Catalyst, and National Pastors Convention. Named one of the "Thirty Emerging Voices" of Christian leaders under age forty by *Charisma* magazine, she has written more than 700 articles and a dozen books, including *The Organic God* and *The Sacred Echo*. She lives in Colorado.

# *From Warrior to Servant*

## Jesus the Messiah (Matthew 16:13–28)

Dr. Matt Williams

Simon Peter answered, "You are the Christ, the Son of the living God."

*⊙ Matthew 16:16*

The way of glory is down the road of suffering.

*⊙ Darrell Bock*

# INTRODUCTION

**Video Opener from Israel**

Cave for the worship of Pan, Greek god of nature, at Caesarea Philippi

**Scripture Reading:** Matthew 16:13–28, followed by a prayer that God will open your heart as you study his Word

**Location of Passage:** Region of Caesarea Philippi

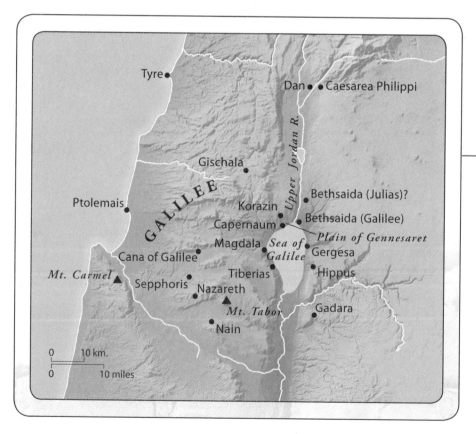

# MAKING DEEPER CONNECTIONS TO THE BIBLE

*Jesus is the powerful Messiah. He can overthrow the Romans, but he came to overthrow a more powerful enemy than Rome.*

## *Video Teaching #1 Notes*

NOTE: In each session of this participant's guide, the "Video Teaching Notes" sections give an outline of the video teaching, with additional quotes and biblical passages. Educators have proved that the teacher's main points will be remembered better if you follow along in the guide and see the main teaching points, and even better if you jot down notes in the spaces provided.

**Location of Video Teaching:** Vulture City Gold Mine, Phoenix, Arizona

The enticement of wealth and power

"Who do people say the Son of Man is?" (Matthew 16:13)

*People hoped Jesus was a prophet*

"Some say John the Baptist" (Matthew 16:14)

"Others say Elijah" (Matthew 16:14)

> See, I will send you the prophet Elijah before that great and dreadful day of the LORD comes.
>
> Malachi 4:5

"Still others [say] Jeremiah or one of the prophets" (Matthew 16:14)

> I will raise up for them a prophet like you [Moses] from among their brothers; I will put my words in his mouth, and he will tell them everything I command him.
>
> Deuteronomy 18:18

"But what about you? Who do you say I am?" (Matthew 16:15)

"You are the Christ, the Son of the living God" (Matthew 16:16)

*Peter Said.*

> So Samuel took the horn of oil and anointed [David] in the presence of his brothers, and from that day on the Spirit of the LORD came upon David in power.
>
> 1 Samuel 16:13

## The Christ

*"The Messiah"*

## Jewish expectations for the Messiah

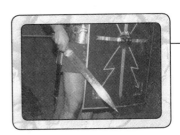

> See, Lord, and raise up for them their king, the son of David, to rule over your servant Israel ... undergird him with the strength to destroy the unrighteous rulers, to purge Jerusalem from Gentiles who trample her to destruction.
>
> Psalms of Solomon 17:21–22

> How fine is the King, the Messiah, who will arise from the house of Judah! He girds his loins and goes forth and sets up the ranks of battle against his enemies and kills the kings.... He reddens the mountains with the blood of their slain and his garments are dipped in blood.
>
> *Targum Yerushalmi* to Genesis 49:11

## Jesus' response to Peter

> Blessed are you, Simon son of Jonah, for this was not revealed to you by man, but by my Father in heaven. And I tell you that you are Peter, and on this rock I will build my church, and the gates of Hades will not overcome it.
>
> Matthew 16:17–18

Peter is the leader of the early church in Jerusalem and a key figure in opening the door to Samaritan and Gentile missions in Acts 8 and 10.

Craig Blomberg

## The gates of Hades

The promise is that even the full fury of the underworld's demonic forces will not overcome the church.

D. A. Carson

## Binding and loosing

*Satan will not overcome the church*

> I will give you the keys of the kingdom of heaven; whatever you bind on earth will be bound in heaven, and whatever you loose on earth will be loosed in heaven.
>
> Matthew 16:19

*Peter chose Keys*

## Keys of the kingdom

*All christians have Keys*

Peter (with keys), Vatican

## Don't tell anyone

Then he warned his disciples not to tell anyone that he was the Christ.

Matthew 16:20

## The turning point

### DID YOU KNOW?

In Jewish life in the time of Jesus, the term "Messiah" had come to mean the expected one whom God would send to deliver Israel and to establish God's righteous role upon the earth.

Larry Hurtado

From that time on Jesus began to explain to his disciples that he must go to Jerusalem and suffer many things at the hands of the elders, chief priests and teachers of the law, and that he must be killed and on the third day be raised to life.

Matthew 16:21

*Turning point*
*Gods will*

## Peter tries to "correct" Jesus, Jesus responds

*Get behind me, Satan*

> Peter took him aside and began to rebuke him. "Never, Lord!" he said. "This shall never happen to you!" Jesus turned and said to Peter, "Get behind me, Satan! You are a stumbling block to me; you do not have in mind the things of God, but the things of men."
>
> Matthew 16:22–23

## Peter does not understand a suffering Messiah

> Jesus was putting together two Old Testament themes that had never been joined together before: the royal, ruling Messiah and the Suffering Servant. It seemed a contradiction in terms, different than anything expected in Judaism.
>
> Peter Walker

## The Old Testament idea of a suffering Messiah

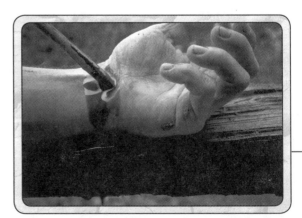

> He was pierced for our transgressions, he was crushed for our iniquities; the punishment that brought us peace was upon him, and by his wounds we are healed. We all, like sheep, have gone astray, each of us has turned to his own way; and the LORD has laid on him the iniquity of us all.
>
> Isaiah 53:5–6

> And I will pour out on the house of David and the inhabitants of Jerusalem a spirit of grace and supplication. They will look on me, the one they have pierced, and they will mourn for him.
>
> Zechariah 12:10

## After the resurrection

> Lord, are you at this time going to restore the kingdom to Israel?
>
> Acts 1:6

## Power

> You will receive power when the Holy Spirit comes on you; and you will be my witnesses in Jerusalem, and in all Judea and Samaria, and to the ends of the earth.
>
> Acts 1:8

## One more surprise

> If anyone would come after me, he must deny himself and take up his cross and follow me.
>
> Matthew 16:24

## Jesus will be raised from the dead

Jesus would not be taking up arms against the Romans; instead his own arms would be stretched out on a Roman cross.

Peter Walker

# VIDEO DISCUSSION #1: MAKING DEEPER CONNECTIONS TO THE BIBLE

NOTE: In each session of the participant's guide, "Video Discussion #1" mainly focuses on understanding the *meaning of the biblical text* in all its depth and fullness. Please see the leader's guide for the amount of time your group should discuss the following questions before moving on to Video Teaching #2, Connecting the Bible to Life.

1. Looking back at the Bible passage and your video teaching notes, what did you learn that you did not know previously? Consider specifically:

   • The different expectations for John the Baptist, Elijah, and Jeremiah to return from the dead

   • The meaning of the term "Christ"

   • Peter's response to Jesus' statement that he was going to suffer and die

   • The Old Testament idea of a suffering Messiah

2. Summarize the Jewish expectations for the Messiah. Do you think that you would have seen Jesus as the Messiah if you had lived at that time? Why or why not?

3. Define as simply as you can the following terms: "gates of Hades," "binding and loosing," and "keys of the kingdom." How would you have felt if you were Peter hearing Jesus tell you these things?

4. Jesus said, "I will build my church and the gates of Hades will not overcome it." Do you think that Jesus has "successfully" built his church in the last two thousand years? Why or why not? Consider the example as China (where the government destroyed all the Bibles, sent home all the missionaries, killed or imprisoned Christian leaders, and yet the church continued to grow) or other instances when the church has faced tremendous opposition.

# CONNECTING THE BIBLE TO LIFE

*Denying myself takes me off the throne and places Christ on the throne of my life every day.*

## *Video Teaching #2 Notes*

God will build his church

> I will build my church, and the gates of Hades will not overcome it.
>
> Matthew 16:18

Who Jesus really is

> If anyone would come after me, he must deny himself and take up his cross and follow me. For whoever wants to save his life will lose it, but whoever loses his life for me will find it.
>
> Matthew 16:24–25

Denying myself

The "good life"

Denying myself is hard

If we wish to follow "in the steps of Jesus," we must remember that those steps lead us inevitably to his cross.

Peter Walker

Is it worth it?

## The rewards

Life lost out of loyalty to Jesus ensures that *true* life is gained.

R. T. France

## The retirement plan

For the Son of Man is going to come in his Father's glory with his angels, and then he will reward each person according to what he has done.

Matthew 16:27

## Suffering for a cause

In this you greatly rejoice, though now for a little while you may have had to suffer grief in all kinds of trials. These have come so that your faith — of greater worth than gold, which perishes even though refined by fire — may be proved genuine and may result in praise, glory and honor when Jesus Christ is revealed.

1 Peter 1:6–7

Jesus has no intention to fill the ranks of his army with volunteers who profess allegiance to him but are unwilling to make sacrifices.

David Garland

# VIDEO DISCUSSION #2: CONNECTING THE BIBLE TO LIFE

NOTE: While "Video Discussion #1" mainly focused on the meaning of the biblical text, "Video Discussion #2" in each session mainly focuses on *applying* the biblical text to our lives today. Please see the leader's guide for the amount of time your group should discuss the following questions.

1. Jesus calls all of us to die to ourselves so that we can serve others. One way to see if you have died to yourself is to see how easily you are offended by others. When was the last time you were offended by someone? What did they do?

2. How do you define the "good life"? Would those who never hear you speak a single word be able to catch that definition by the life that you live? Give an example or two of what they would see.

3. Do you think that sacrificing in order to serve God and others is worth it? Why or why not?

*Ecclesia*

4. Dead people have released everything—they simply cannot take anything with them. As living-dead people, we continually face the battle of releasing all to the Lord, realizing that we are stewards, not owners. What is there in your life that you have not yet released? Not long ago, a California wildfire came within a half mile of destroying our home. What would your attitude be if you lost every possession in a situation like that?

# MAKING DEEPER CONNECTIONS IN YOUR OWN LIFE

*Personal reflection studies to do on your own*

## Day One

1. Read Mark 8:27–38, then compare it to the Matthew 16:13–28 account.

2. How do you think that Jesus builds his church today? Does he work through people or does he do it on his own? What is the relationship between divine work and our own responsibility?

3. Peter certainly sacrificed for the gospel—not only in his life, but in his cruel death on a cross, hanging upside down. How many stories have you heard about missionaries sacrificing for the gospel? Should those who are not called to the mission field also sacrifice for the gospel? If so, what would that look like?

# Day Two

1.  Read Luke 9:18–27. Compare it to the Matthew and Mark accounts.

2.  Some people devote themselves to gaining the whole world, yet do not find fulfillment even when they "reach the top." To what do you devote your life? Have you found rewards from this devotion? Spend some time in prayer on this topic.

3.  Think once more about your own definition of the "good life." Is it relaxing on a beach, having a big house, wearing the latest fashions? Or is it found in sacrificing your own wants for the needs of others—in service? What do you have your eye on that keeps your eyes from being more fully on God?

# Day Three

1. Read John 1:36–42. If the disciples did not understand what kind of Messiah Jesus was in Matthew 16, what do you think they understood about Jesus' messiahship in John 1, after just meeting him?

2. It is very important to fully understand who Jesus is so that we can follow him wholeheartedly. Who do you think Jesus really is? Who is he *for you*? List below attributes of his character along with actions either from the gospel record or your own life that help you to confirm your belief.

3. There certainly was a difference of opinion between what the Jewish crowds thought of the Messiah in comparison to what Jesus taught—the difference between reigning and suffering/ serving. What does popular opinion say about being a follower of Jesus today? Do you agree with it? In your Christian community, do you hear more about reigning/blessing or about suffering/serving?

# Day Four

1. Read Luke 14:25–27.

2. What specific ways can you think of to sacrifice yourself to serve others? List as many as you can here.

3. Just as Peter was a stumbling block to Jesus' path, how do we limit Jesus in our lives? How do you, like Peter, project your self-interests and aspirations on Jesus?

# Day Five

1. Read Matthew 16:13–28 one more time.

2. Pray through the entire passage verse by verse, allowing the deeper meaning that you have discovered to lead you as you pray. Ask the Spirit to continue to remind you of what you have learned and to help you apply these truths to your life. Jot down any further applications that come to mind as you pray.

3. Turn back to the discussion questions from the video teaching (Video Discussion #1, #2). If there are questions that your group did not have time to discuss or questions that you might like to think more about, use this time to review and reflect further.

## A Glimpse of Glory

### The Transfiguration
### (Matthew 17:1–9)

Prof. Susan Hecht

There he was transfigured before them. His face shone like the sun, and his clothes became as white as the light.

*⊚ Matthew 17:2*

Heaven has invaded earth and the superhuman glory of the Messiah has been revealed.

*⊚ R. T. France*

# INTRODUCTION

**Video Opener from Israel**

Mount Hermon

**Scripture Reading:** Matthew 17:1–9, followed by a prayer that God will open your heart as you study his Word

**Location of Passage:** Perhaps Mount Hermon (near Caesarea Philippi, twenty-five miles north of the Sea of Galilee)

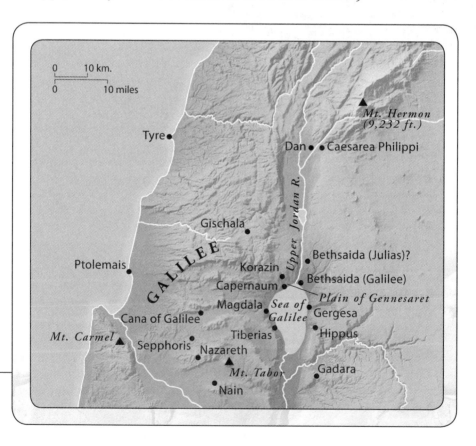

# MAKING DEEPER CONNECTIONS TO THE BIBLE

*The Transfiguration gave the disciples a glimpse of who Jesus really is.*

## *Video Teaching #1 Notes*

**Location of Video Teaching:** Pikes Peak, Colorado

A divine sight

> After six days Jesus took with him Peter, James and John the brother of James, and led them up a high mountain by themselves. There he was transfigured before them. His face shone like the sun, and his clothes became as white as the light. Just then there appeared before them Moses and Elijah, talking with Jesus.
>
> Matthew 17:1–3

Moses and Elijah

### DID YOU KNOW?

Bright, shining, or white clothing often symbolizes purity and victory and is associated in Jewish apocalyptic writing with the coming of Messiah.

Doug Moo

## Peter's inappropriate response

> Peter said to Jesus, "Lord, it is good for us to be here. If you wish, I will put up three shelters — one for you, one for Moses and one for Elijah."
>
> Matthew 17:4

## A bright cloud: God's response to Peter

In the hall of fame that is made up of the great figures of the Bible, no one occupies a space alongside Jesus; he is unique.

Darrell Bock

## A divine response

> While he was still speaking, a bright cloud enveloped them, and a voice from the cloud said, "This is my Son, whom I love; with him I am well pleased. Listen to him!"
>
> Matthew 17:5

## "Listen to him!"

> The LORD your God will raise up for you a prophet like me from among your own brothers. You must listen to him.
>
> Deuteronomy 18:15

### DID YOU KNOW?

The imperative "listen" may mean more than just "hear." The Hebrew term often means "obey."

W. D. Davies

## An appropriate response by the disciples

When the disciples heard this, they fell facedown to the ground, terrified. But Jesus came and touched them. "Get up," he said. "Don't be afraid." When they looked up, they saw no one except Jesus.

Matthew 17:6–8

Touch is important because it communicates security and love.

IVP Women's Bible Commentary

## What is this passage about?

Jesus will take the same three disciples with him to another hillside at the foot of the Mount of Olives — Gethsemane. This time, however, they will see a man in tears and deep distress.

Peter Walker

The context before the transfiguration

Simon Peter answered, "You are the Christ, the Son of the living God."

Matthew 16:16

The end of the transfiguration

As they were coming down the mountain, Jesus instructed them, "Don't tell anyone what you have seen, until the Son of Man has been raised from the dead."

Matthew 17:9

## The context after the transfiguration: Matthew 17:23 and Acts

### *The Wizard of Oz* in reverse

Many in the church remember only the parts of the Bible that promise wealth, happiness, and glory and forget the calls for self-sacrifice. They want to skip Suffering 101 and move on to advanced placement in Glory 909.

David Garland

The transfiguration gives them a glimpse of his divine nature, to help them to understand that even though Jesus the Messianic King must go to Jerusalem to suffer and die (Matthew 16), he will be raised again.

Susan Hecht

# VIDEO DISCUSSION #1: MAKING DEEPER CONNECTIONS TO THE BIBLE

1. Looking back at the Bible passage and your video teaching notes, what did you learn that you did not know previously? Consider specifically:

   • The appearance of Jesus during the transfiguration

   • Peter's response to the transfiguration

   • God's message from the cloud

2. Susan Hecht talked about the fact that the transfiguration came immediately after Jesus' announcement that he would not be a reigning Messiah, but a suffering Messiah (Matthew 16:21). Do you think that this is relevant to the meaning of the transfiguration? What do you think Jesus was trying to teach his disciples through this event?

3. God's voice announced, "This is my Son, whom I love; with him I am well pleased." Why do you think that God was "well pleased" with Jesus? Do you think that he is well pleased with you? Why or why not? Is it possible to make God more "pleased"?

4. Matthew 17:6 states that when the disciples heard God's command, they fell on their faces and were filled with awe. Why is this an appropriate response? When do you think such a response would be appropriate today?

# CONNECTING THE BIBLE TO LIFE

*Jesus is who he said he is, and one day all things will be made right.*

## Video Teaching #2 Notes

Jesus: name above all names

The present-day church needs once again to discover the absolute authority of the teaching of Jesus.

Donald Hagner

Putting Jesus before everything else

> What is more, I consider everything a loss compared to the surpassing greatness of knowing Christ Jesus my Lord, for whose sake I have lost all things. I consider them rubbish, that I may gain Christ.
>
> Philippians 3:8

## "Get up; don't be afraid"

> Your enemy the devil prowls around like a roaring lion looking for someone to devour.
>
> 1 Peter 5:8

Seeking transfigurational
moments

Peter: the transfiguration
motivated him

> We ourselves heard this voice that came from heaven when we were with him
> on the sacred mountain.
>
> 2 Peter 1:18

## Live *now*, knowing that Jesus is coming back

The glory glimpsed in the transfiguration scene is a precious reality
not to be doubted, but as a manifest reality it belongs to the other
side of suffering.

John Nolland

## Climbing a mountain in Colorado

"It's worth it"

The dullness of earthly conditions was temporarily stripped away, so that the true nature of God's "beloved Son" can for once be seen.

R. T. France

## Difficult, but worth it

Be all the more eager to make your calling and election sure. For if you do these things, you will never fall, and you will receive a rich welcome into the eternal kingdom of our Lord and Savior Jesus Christ.

2 Peter 1:10–11

In spite of the terrible suffering, Christians will be glorified with Jesus.

David Garland

# VIDEO DISCUSSION #2: CONNECTING THE BIBLE TO LIFE

1. Even though Jesus the Messiah suffered and died (contrary to Jewish expectations of a conquering warrior Messiah), the transfiguration gave the disciples a glimpse of his glory. How might this experience have helped keep them going, to the point of suffering and eventually being martyred for him? If you had been there on the mountain with Jesus, do you think it would have been enough to keep you from leaving him?

2. Have you gotten a glimpse of Jesus' glory? What did it look like? What are other ways that one could gain a glimpse of Jesus' glory today?

3. Though we seek transformational moments of glory where we see God, Jesus, and the Spirit in all their fullness, we normally live in the mundane existence of daily life. Is it discouraging for you to not experience more transfigurational moments than you do? What if you don't get one? Does it change anything?

4. In the midst of difficulties, including pressure to compromise our Christian faith and obedience to God, does recognizing the true nature of Jesus' glory and the fact that he will return one day influence decisions you make on a day-to-day basis? If so, how? If not, why not?

# MAKING DEEPER CONNECTIONS IN YOUR OWN LIFE

*Personal reflection studies to do on your own*

## Day One

1. Read Mark 9:2–10. Note any similarities and differences compared with Matthew 17:1–9.

2. Despite the fact that the disciples were having a hard time grasping what God was showing them, he still commanded them—and apparently expected them—to listen to Jesus and obey him. How does this provide an example for us today? How do you tend to respond when you don't understand what God is doing in a particular situation?

3. Transfigurational moments can take place when we pray, meditate on the Word, or fellowship with other Christians. In what practical ways can you focus on Jesus and listen to him *now* to prepare you for difficult times in the *future*? Spend some time in prayer asking him to speak to you now, in the present, about those difficult things that you see in your future.

# Day Two

1. Read Luke 9:28–36. Note any similarities and differences compared with Matthew 17:1–9.

2. Matthew says that Jesus was "transfigured" before the disciples' eyes. Paul uses this same word in Romans 12:2 and 2 Corinthians 3:18 to describe the spiritual change that believers experience, though in those verses the word is translated "transformed." Do you think that Christians can be "transformed" into something new by God's grace and power? Have you seen that happen in your life? Thank God in prayer for the changes you can see, and give him permission to continue the transformation process. Note below any areas that you feel the Lord is speaking to you about as you pray.

3. Jesus did not give up on the disciples, even when they didn't get it, even when they were afraid. He was patient with them in their growth process. Do you think that the Lord is just as patient with you? Are you as patient with yourself as Jesus is with you? Thank him for his patience with you, and ask him to give you more patience with yourself as you continue to be transformed into his likeness.

# Day Three

1. Read Luke 24:13–35.

2. God's voice from the cloud said, "This is my Son, whom I love; with him I am well pleased. Listen to him!" (Matthew 17:5). Not only is Jesus the Messiah, but he is also the Lord who teaches us right from wrong. How well do you think you know Jesus' teachings? How healthy is your spiritual discipline of reading, meditating on, and memorizing Scripture?

3. On the road to Emmaus, Jesus spoke to two of his disciples without them knowing who he was. When they finally figured out his identity, they said, "Were not our hearts burning within us while he talked with us?" (Luke 24:32). What do you think they meant? Have you ever felt your "heart burning within you" as you spent time in prayer or in God's Word?

# Day Four

1. Read 2 Peter 1:12–18.

2. When Peter wrote this epistle, he was near the end of his life yet he referred to the transfiguration, which happened years before. Why do you think Peter would mention this event? What assurances did the transfiguration give him? As you grow older, how important is it to be assured both of the reality of Jesus' glory and the trustworthiness of the traditions that have been passed down to us?

3. Why do you think the transfiguration frightened the disciples? What makes you afraid? Just as Jesus came to the disciples in their fear and told them, "Get up, don't be afraid," he desires the same for you. As you pray today, give your fears to Jesus; ask him to "touch" you and take them away.

# Day Five

1. Read Matthew 17:1–9 one more time.

2. Pray through the entire passage verse by verse, allowing the deeper meaning that you have discovered to lead you as you pray. Ask the Spirit to continue to remind you of what you have learned and to help you apply these truths to your life. Jot down any further applications that come to mind as you pray.

3. Turn back to the discussion questions from the video teaching (Video Discussion #1, #2). If there are questions that your group did not have time to discuss or questions that you might like to think more about, use this time to review and reflect further.

# The Rejected King

## The Triumphal Entry (Matthew 21:1–22)

Dr. Mark Strauss

Say to the Daughter of Zion,
"See, your king comes to you,
gentle and riding on a donkey,
on a colt, the foal of a donkey."

*Matthew 21:5*

He comes as a king who will be
crowned with thorns, enthroned
on a cross.

*David Garland*

# INTRODUCTION

**Video Opener from Israel**

Descent down the
Mount of Olives

**Scripture Reading:** Matthew 21:1–22,
followed by a prayer that God will open
your heart as you study his Word

**Location of Passage:** Mount of Olives, Jerusalem Temple

# MAKING DEEPER CONNECTIONS TO THE BIBLE

*After centuries of longing and waiting for their savior, the Messiah, he
has arrived. Jesus is about to enter Jerusalem.*

## Video Teaching #1 Notes

**Location of Video Teaching:** Kay El Bar dude ranch, Phoenix, Arizona

The triumphal entry on Palm Sunday

### DID YOU KNOW?

The spreading of garments
and palm branches on
the road marks the festive
acknowledgment of Jesus'
kingship.

David Turner

The context in Matthew

Feast of Passover

> ## DID YOU KNOW?
>
> In the time of Jesus, the Mount of Olives was, as its name implies, a hill covered with olive groves, but these were destroyed by the Roman forces besieging Jerusalem in AD 70.
>
> Peter Walker

Jesus enters Jerusalem humbly

> Rejoice greatly, O Daughter of Zion!... See, your king comes to you, righteous and having salvation, gentle and riding on a donkey, on a colt, the foal of a donkey."
>
> Zechariah 9:9

## Jesus enters as the messianic king

The crowds that went ahead of him and those that followed shouted, "Hosanna to the Son of David! Blessed is he who comes in the name of the Lord! Hosanna in the highest!"

Matthew 21:9

His entrance points to a different kind of triumph than the one envisioned by the crowd, one that will be more powerful than any Davidic monarchy and more far-reaching than even the Roman Empire.

David Garland

## Bad news: Jewish leaders reject Jesus

But when the chief priests and the teachers of the law saw the wonderful things he did and the children shouting in the temple area, "Hosanna to the Son of David," they were indignant.

Matthew 21:15

## Jesus' cleansing of the temple

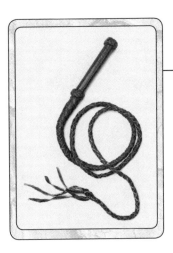

> My house will be called a house of prayer [Isaiah 56:7], but you are making it a den of robbers [Jeremiah 7:11].
>
> Matthew 21:13

## A judgment of the temple

> O Jerusalem, Jerusalem, you who kill the prophets and stone those sent to you, how often I have longed to gather your children together, as a hen gathers her chicks under her wings, but you were not willing. Look, your house is left to you desolate.
>
> Matthew 23:37–38

Judgment brings Jesus pain. He weeps for Jerusalem as he thinks about her suffering.

Darrell Bock

# The children understand

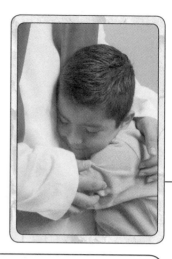

From the lips of children and infants you have ordained praise.

Matthew 21:16 (see Psalm 8:2)

# Jesus' cursing of the fig tree, its symbolism

"May you never bear fruit again!" Immediately the tree withered.

Matthew 21:19b

Jesus' actions are deliberate, designed to draw attention and to provoke people to think about his messianic claims.

R. T. France

# VIDEO DISCUSSION #1: MAKING DEEPER CONNECTIONS TO THE BIBLE

1. We normally call Jesus' arrival in Jerusalem the "triumphal entry." Do you think that it was a triumphant entry? Why or why not? How did Jesus triumph in Jerusalem? In what ways did he not triumph?

2. When Mark Strauss mentioned that the Jewish leaders did not rejoice at Jesus' triumphal entry, but rejected him instead, were you surprised? In other words, does it surprise you that the Jewish leaders did not accept Jesus as their Messiah? Why or why not?

3. All three of these Matthew 21 events (the triumphal entry, the cleansing of the temple, and the cursing of the fig tree) need to be read and interpreted together in order to understand the deeper meaning. Does it surprise you that these events talk about judgment? Do you think it was easy or hard for Jesus to announce judgment on Jerusalem? Do you think it is easy or hard for him to announce judgment upon those today who do not accept him as Messiah?

4. Why do you think that the children in the temple praised Jesus?
   What did they see in him that the Jewish leaders did not? Do
   you think it is easier for a child to accept Jesus as the true
   Messiah? Why or why not?

   *Jesus takes care of the children*

# CONNECTING THE BIBLE TO LIFE

*We are all like those pilgrims watching Jesus enter Jerusalem. Jesus
comes down the road, but how will we respond?*

## Video Teaching #2 Notes

Jesus came to serve

> A donkey now bears him as king as he enters Jerusalem; soon he will
> bear his own cross as he is kicked out of Jerusalem.
>
> Darrell Bock

God is calling us to this self-sacrificial service

We are responsible to God for fruit

> Seeing a fig tree by the road, [Jesus] went up to it but found nothing on it except leaves.
>
> Matthew 21:19a

## God's vision for the world

## How will you respond?

Here is what is at stake for Israel when Jesus comes: peace or judgment. This is a picture of the choice that Jesus' ministry leaves for everyone.

Darrell Bock

# VIDEO DISCUSSION #2: CONNECTING THE BIBLE TO LIFE

1. If you had been in Jerusalem when Jesus entered the city, do you think you would have responded like: the crowds (Matthew 21:8–9), the Jewish leaders (21:15), the children (21:15–16), or the fig tree (21:19)? Explain your answer.

2. Mark Strauss says that God has called us to self-sacrificial service. Why do you think it is necessary to couple sacrifice with service? Can't we serve others without sacrificing?

3. List all the ways that you currently serve other people. Start with types of service within the church, then expand it to include service to your community, then expand it to include serving the entire world. What are some other ways that you could serve these same groups of people?

4. Jesus judged those in Jerusalem who failed to bear fruit. Remembering that John the Baptist called for repentance *and* a change of action (Luke 3:7–14), do you think Jesus was looking for the same thing, or did he just want people to "accept him into their hearts"? Explain. How would most Christians that you know answer this question?

# MAKING DEEPER CONNECTIONS IN YOUR OWN LIFE

*Personal reflection studies to do on your own*

## Day One

1. Read Mark 11:1–26. Compare this account with Matthew 21:1–22.

2. Jesus entered Jerusalem humbly and in peace, but he could have shown up on a war horse to announce judgment on the Jewish people for their sin. What about us? What does it mean for us to enter our workplaces, our schools, and our communities "triumphantly"? What does it mean to act humbly and in peace in our day-to-day lives?

3. Reflect further on how you would have responded had you been in Jerusalem when Jesus entered (like the crowds, the children, the leaders, or the fig tree). Or, would your reaction have been some combination of these? As you pray today, ask God to help you be the kind of person who responds to Jesus in praise and adoration instead of with indignation or a lack of fruit.

# Day Two

1. Read Jeremiah 7:1–15 and Isaiah 56:3–8.

2. Jewish people in Jeremiah's day (and in Jesus' day) were involved in sins such as stealing, murder, perjury, and idolatry. Perhaps your sins are not as blatant as these, but certainly you struggle with sin at some level. Ask Jesus to "cleanse" your temple—the temple of your heart and body. Ask the Spirit to flow through you and bring purity at every level.

3. The cleansing of the temple was also about the inclusion of outsiders. What about you? You are now the temple of the Lord (1 Corinthians 3:16). Do you include outsiders in your spheres of influence (work, school, community)? Are you the type of person who reaches out to others with the love of God, or are you the type of person who is judgmental and closes off access to God through your lifestyle?

# Day Three

1. Read Luke 19:28–48, then compare it to the Matthew and Mark accounts.

2. In cursing the fig tree (Matthew 21:18–19), Jesus was symbolically cursing Israel. Why? If Jesus came to your church, would he find fruit or not? List below the types of fruit that Jesus would find in your church.

3. Now, let's make this a little more personal. If Jesus came to *you*, would he find fruit in your life or not? List below the types of fruit that Jesus would find. Then pray, asking Jesus, the Vine, to produce more fruit in your life. Record below any impressions you get as you pray—noting fruit that the Lord is asking you to produce, or fruit that he is happy to already see growing in your life.

## Day Four

1. Read John 12:12–19. What differences do you see in this account compared with Matthew's, Mark's, and Luke's?

2. The Jewish people in Jesus' day were looking for a messiah who would set them free from Roman oppression. People today also look for many things from Jesus the Messiah, some of which he provides, many of which he does not. Do you serve Jesus regardless of whether or not he meets your own personal expectations? Why or why not? Do you serve him for what you can get ... or for what you can give?

3. The judgment that Jesus announced that day in Jerusalem was real, inevitable, painful, and tragic. In the future, a day of judgment is coming for *everyone*. The reality of such judgment should motivate us to reach out to those who do not know Christ. As we do, we should remember that God does not win by sending armies into bloody battles but by sending his Son to the cross. He wins when we sacrificially go in his name to bring good news to others. How are you spreading the good news in your life and thus helping others to avoid the day of judgment?

# Day Five

1. Read Matthew 21:1–22 one more time.

2. Pray through the entire passage verse by verse, allowing the deeper meaning that you have discovered to lead you as you pray. Ask the Spirit to continue to remind you of what you have learned and to help you apply these truths to your life. Jot down any further applications that come to mind as you pray.

3. Turn back to the discussion questions from the video teaching (Video Discussion #1, #2). If there are questions that your group did not have time to discuss or questions that you might like to think more about, use this time to review and reflect further.

# Love to the Full

## The Last Supper
(John 13:1–5;
Matthew 26:21–29)

Dr. Scott Duvall

Then he took the cup, gave thanks and offered it to them, saying, "Drink from it, all of you. This is my blood of the covenant, which is poured out for many for the forgiveness of sins."

*Matthew 26:27–28*

At the Last Supper, Jesus interprets his death as the sacrifice that will establish the new covenant predicted in Jeremiah 31.

*Mark Strauss*

# INTRODUCTION

**Video Opener from Israel**

Traditional location of the upper room

**Scripture Reading:** John 13:1–5 and Matthew 26:21–29, followed by a prayer that God will open your heart as you study his Word

**Location of Passage:** The upper room, Jerusalem

# MAKING DEEPER CONNECTIONS TO THE BIBLE

*The Lord's Supper celebrates what Jesus has done in the past for his followers, but it also anticipates what he will do in the future.*

## *Video Teaching #1 Notes*

**Location of Video Teaching:** Plantation, Little Rock, Arkansas

Jesus became like a slave to liberate others

## Jesus loved his disciples

It was just before the Passover Feast. Jesus knew that the time had come for him to leave this world and go to the Father. Having loved his own who were in the world, he now showed them the full extent of his love.

John 13:1

## Jesus shares a Passover meal

Go into the city, and a man carrying a jar of water will meet you. Follow him.... He will show you a large upper room, furnished and ready. Make preparations for us there.

Mark 14:13, 15

## Jesus washes the disciples' feet

This was a model of unbelievable love, to wash the feet of the very one who would send him to his death!

Grant Osborne

## Humility in the Greco-Roman and Jewish world

## Peter

> "No," said Peter, "you shall never wash my feet." Jesus answered, "Unless I wash you, you have no part with me." "Then, Lord," Simon Peter replied, "not just my feet but my hands and my head as well!"
>
> John 13:8–9

## Those with power become servants

> Do you understand what I have done for you?... You call me "Teacher" and "Lord," and rightly so, for that is what I am. Now that I, your Lord and Teacher, have washed your feet, you also should wash one another's feet. I have set you an example that you should do as I have done for you. I tell you the truth, no servant is greater than his master, nor is a messenger greater than the one who sent him. Now that you know these things, you will be blessed if you do them.
>
> John 13:12–17

## Jesus also cleansed their souls

> Your attitude should be the same as that of Christ Jesus: who, being in very nature God, did not consider equality with God something to be grasped, but made himself nothing, taking the very nature of a servant, being made in human likeness. And being found in appearance as a man, he humbled himself and became obedient to death — even death on a cross!
>
> Philippians 2:5–8

## Promised blessing

## One of the Twelve will betray Jesus

> And while they were eating, [Jesus] said, "I tell you the truth, one of you will betray me." They were very sad and began to say to him one after the other, "Surely not I, Lord?"
>
> Matthew 26:21–22

In different ways, all the disciples betray Jesus, not just Judas.

IVP Women's Bible Commentary

## Judas

Even my close friend, whom I trusted, he who shared my bread, has lifted up his heel against me.

Psalm 41:9

—————————— ☉ ——————————

Then Judas, the one who would betray him, said, "Surely not I, Rabbi?" Jesus answered, "Yes, it is you."

Matthew 26:25

## The Passover

### DID YOU KNOW?

The Passover lamb was eaten with bitter herbs (to symbolize the bitterness of slavery in Egypt) and unleavened bread (to symbolize the haste with which they left Egypt).

Mark Strauss

Then they are to take some of the blood and put it on the sides and tops of the doorframes of the houses where they eat the lambs.... On that same night I will pass through Egypt and strike down every firstborn — both men and animals — and I will bring judgment on all the gods of Egypt. I am the LORD. The blood will be a sign for you on the houses where you are; and when I see the blood, I will pass over you. No destructive plague will touch you when I strike Egypt.

Exodus 12:7, 12–13

## The Lord's Supper

| | |
|---|---|
| Slavery in Egypt | Slavery to sin |
| God's deliverance through Passover lamb | God's deliverance through Jesus |
| Exodus from Egypt | Forgiveness of sins |
| Covenant at Mount Sinai | New covenant through Jesus' blood |
| Passover | Lord's Supper |

"This is my body" (Matthew 26:26)

Unleavened and leavened bread

### DID YOU KNOW?

In the Passover meal, a portion of the unleavened bread was broken off with the understanding that the Messiah would eat it when he comes and celebrates with Israel. Jesus distributed this portion to his disciples and declares, "This is my body." Jesus has identified himself as the Messiah.

Craig Evans

"This is my blood of the covenant, which is poured out for many for the forgiveness of sins" (Matthew 26:28)

"The time is coming," declares the LORD, "when I will make a new covenant with the house of Israel and with the house of Judah.... I will put my law in their minds and write it on their hearts. I will be their God, and they will be my people.... I will forgive their wickedness and will remember their sins no more."

Jeremiah 31:31, 33–34

"I will not drink of this fruit of the vine from now on until that day when I drink it anew with you in my Father's kingdom" (Matthew 26:29)

### DID YOU KNOW?

The cup was an Old Testament picture for the "wrath of the Lord," which God required his enemies to drink. Now Jesus drinks from the cup of judgment, so that his followers would never need to.

Peter Walker

"Do this in remembrance of me" (Luke 22:19)

The call to "remember" is Jewish, which the nation did annually in the Passover as they looked back at the Exodus.

Darrell Bock

Jesus' final words (John 14–17)

## VIDEO DISCUSSION #1: MAKING DEEPER CONNECTIONS TO THE BIBLE

1. If you had lived in the first century, would it have surprised you that Jesus, the Master and Lord, humbled himself, became like a slave, and washed his disciples' feet? Do you think that most Christians today are quick to humble themselves? Why or why not?

2. How would you have reacted if you had been present at the Last Supper and it came time to let Jesus wash your feet? Would you have let him? Why or why not?

3. How does the background of the Passover help you understand the deeper meaning of the Lord's Supper?

4. Which of the four sayings of Jesus at the supper is most meaningful to you? Why?

# CONNECTING THE BIBLE TO LIFE

*Jesus is the supreme example of humility, and we should follow that example by serving others.*

## *Video Teaching #2 Notes*

Jesus loves the world

The footwashing is a parable in action, setting out that great principle of lowly service which brings cleansing and which finds its supreme embodiment in the cross.

Leon Morris

Selfless love

True humility serves others

Religion that God our Father accepts as pure and faultless is this: to look after orphans and widows in their distress and to keep oneself from being polluted by the world.

James 1:27

Forgiveness

"The time is coming," declares the LORD, "when I will make a new covenant with the house of Israel and with the house of Judah.... I will forgive their wickedness and will remember their sins no more."

Jeremiah 31:31, 34

Since we have a great priest ... let us draw near to God with a sincere heart in full assurance of faith, having our hearts sprinkled to cleanse us from a guilty conscience.

Hebrews 10:21–22

## Let God love you

## Let God forgive you

> If we confess our sins, he is faithful and just and will forgive us our sins and purify us from all unrighteousness.
>
> 1 John 1:9

## Free from the slavery to sin

> But thanks be to God that, though you used to be slaves to sin ... you have been set free from sin.
>
> Romans 6:17–18

The Lord's Supper is a perpetual reminder of the new and greater exodus by which all who embrace its significance find release from sin's bondage.

Michael Wilkins

# VIDEO DISCUSSION #2: CONNECTING THE BIBLE TO LIFE

1. Who are some humble servants you know? What do they do to serve like Jesus?

2. When do you find it most difficult to let God love you? What helps you allow God's love to penetrate your heart? (If time permits, as a group pray briefly to celebrate God's love for you.)

3. God instructs us to confess our sins to receive forgiveness. Why does that seem too easy at times and too difficult at others? What kinds of things do we sometimes substitute for confessing? What should we do when we struggle to forgive ourselves?

# MAKING DEEPER CONNECTIONS IN YOUR OWN LIFE

*Personal reflection studies to do on your own*

## Day One

1. Read Ezekiel 34:11–16, 22–31.

2. Focus today on Scott Duvall's application to "let God love us." As you read Ezekiel 34, did you notice how many times God says "I will"? It is very clear that he cares deeply for his people and will do all he can to take care of them. Skim Ezekiel 34 and list all of the promises that God makes concerning you and his care for you.

3. Now spend some time in prayer on each item in your list, thanking God that he cares for you—that he loves you. Take to him any doubts that you have about his love for you, and ask him to flood your heart with his love. Don't rush through this prayer time; sit in the Father's presence and ask him to be *your* Shepherd.

# Day Two

1. Read Hebrews 4:14–5:5.

2. Focus today on Scott Duvall's application to "let God forgive us." Are you quick to go to God for forgiveness, or are you like the college students in the video who are hesitant to go to God because they don't think that they are worthy? Does the Hebrews passage help you to accept that Jesus understands you? Which verses in particular? As you reflect back on your life so far, are there sins for which you have never asked God for forgiveness? Are there sins that you have asked for forgiveness, but you still carry the shame? List below whatever comes to mind.

3. Now spend some time in prayer on each item in your list, thanking God that he cares for you so much that he willingly and gladly forgives you. Take to him any doubts that you have about being truly forgiven, and ask him to flood your heart with his forgiveness. Don't rush through this prayer time; sit in the Father's presence and ask him to be *your* Great High Priest who understands you and offered sacrifice for *your* sins.

# Day Three

1. Read Romans 6:1–14.

2. Focus today on Scott Duvall's application that God wants to "set us free from slavery to sin." Not only did Jesus die to forgive us of our sins, but he set us free from sin itself. Though we will never be sinless this side of heaven, with God's help we can sin less and less. Make a list of those areas of your life where you feel that you could use some extra strength and power from God to overcome sin patterns. As you read Romans 6, what verses really speak to you about these sin patterns?

3. Now spend some time in prayer on each item in your list, thanking God that he cares for you so much that he sent the Spirit to empower you to overcome sin in your life. Take to him any doubts that you have about his power for you, and ask him to flood your heart with the Spirit's power. Don't rush through this prayer time; sit in the Father's presence and ask him to be *your* Strength.

# Day Four

1. Read John 13.

2. How do you react when you're betrayed by a friend? Can you imagine what Jesus experienced at the Last Supper, knowing that within hours one of the Twelve would hand him over to be killed? Would you want to share food with Judas? Would you want to wash his feet? What are some specific ways that we can respond more like Jesus did at his betrayal?

3. Do you think we should observe foot washing in our local churches today? If so, what practical guidelines would you suggest? If not, can you think of equivalent practices that demonstrate humble service in our day? Who could you humbly serve this week?

# Day Five

1. Read John 13:1–5 and Matthew 26:21–29 one more time.

2. Pray through the entire passage verse by verse, allowing the deeper meaning that you have discovered to lead you as you pray. Ask the Spirit to continue to remind you of what you have learned and to help you apply these truths to your life. Jot down any further applications that come to mind as you pray.

3. Turn back to the discussion questions from the video teaching (Video Discussion #1, #2). If there are questions that your group did not have time to discuss or questions that you might like to think more about, use this time to review and reflect further.

## *The Ultimate Victory*

# The Trial and Death of Jesus
## (Luke 22:66–23:3; 23:32–34, 44–47)

Dr. Darrell Bock

When they came to the place called the Skull, there they crucified him.

*Luke 23:33*

This was a death that dealt with human sin, absorbing its full force and removing its judgment, so that people could experience God's love and forgiveness.

*Peter Walker*

# INTRODUCTION

**Video Opener from Israel**

Golgotha (the "Skull"), possible site of Jesus' crucifixion

**Scripture Reading:** Luke 22:66–23:3; 23:32–34, 44–47, followed by a prayer that God will open your heart as you study his Word

**Location of Passage:** Jerusalem; ancient tradition says that Jesus was crucified and buried in what is now the Church of the Holy Sepulchre, though others point to Golgotha and the Garden Tomb

Church of the Holy Sepulchre, traditional location of Jesus' tomb

# MAKING DEEPER CONNECTIONS TO THE BIBLE

*Jesus is not just a great teacher who goes to the cross. He is the Son of Man who will sit at the right hand of the Father.*

## Video Teaching #1 Notes

**Location of Video Teaching:** Dealey Plaza, Dallas, Texas

Jesus entered Jerusalem

The events that led to Jesus' death

Crucifixion

**DID YOU KNOW?**

Crucifixion was thought to be so disgusting by some Romans that the use of the word for "cross" was banned as a topic of conversation in polite Roman society.

Peter Walker

Jesus before the Jewish leaders

Jesus was the victim of lies and innuendo, frame-ups, and a rigged jury.

David Garland

"Are you the Christ?"

## Jesus' answer: at the right hand of the Father

> **DID YOU KNOW?**
>
> Jesus' answer that the Son of Man will be sitting at the right hand of God in power implies that he is on the same level with God.
>
> David Garland

> "Yes, it is as you say," Jesus replied. "But I say to all of you: In the future you will see the Son of Man sitting at the right hand of the Mighty One and coming on the clouds of heaven."
>
> Matthew 26:64

## Riding the clouds

## Sharing glory with God the Father

## Moses

> **Moses:** I had a vision of a great throne on the top of Mount Sinai ... I approached and stood before the throne. He gave me the scepter and instructed me to sit on the great throne. Then he gave me a royal crown.
>
> *Exagoge of Ezekiel 67–90*

## Son of Man

When they see that *Son of Man* sitting on the throne of his glory.

1 Enoch 62:5

## God shares his glory with no one

## Metatron

All these things the Holy One, blessed be he, made for me: He made me a Throne, similar to the Throne of Glory ... and seated me on it. And the herald went forth into every Heaven, saying: "This is Metatron, my Vice Regent, my servant and my spouse. I have made him into a prince and a ruler over all the princes of my kingdoms."

3 Enoch 10:1–3

Rabbi Akiba: David

Jesus' claim is offensive

The high priest's response

> The high priest tore his clothes. "Why do we need any more witnesses?" he asked. "You have heard the blasphemy. What do you think?" They all condemned him as worthy of death.
>
> Mark 14:63–64

A train wreck in the making

The religious charge is turned into a political charge

> Pilate was responsible for ensuring that order was maintained and for deciding the death penalty.
>
> David Garland

The charges before Pilate

> Then the whole assembly rose and led him off to Pilate. And they began to accuse him, saying, "We have found this man subverting our nation. He opposes payment of taxes to Caesar and claims to be Christ, a king."
>
> Luke 23:1–2

## Pilate thinks Jesus is innocent

> Then Pilate announced to the chief priests and the crowd, "I find no basis for a charge against this man."
>
> Luke 23:4
>
> ───────────── ◎ ─────────────
>
> "Crucify him!" they shouted. "Why? What crime has he committed?" asked Pilate. But they shouted all the louder, "Crucify him!" Wanting to satisfy the crowd, Pilate released Barabbas to them. He had Jesus flogged, and handed him over to be crucified.
>
> Mark 15:13–15

## Pilate orders Jesus to be crucified

> Pilate had a notice prepared and fastened to the cross. It read: JESUS OF NAZARETH, THE KING OF THE JEWS.... The chief priests of the Jews protested to Pilate, "Do not write 'The King of the Jews,' but that this man claimed to be king of the Jews." Pilate answered, "What I have written, I have written."
>
> John 19:19, 21–22

Jewish context of Jesus' claim
to sit at the right hand

Jesus claims that God will vindicate him

Jesus replied, "But I say to all of you: In the future you will see the Son of Man sitting at the right hand of the Mighty One and coming on the clouds of heaven."

Matthew 26:64

The empty tomb vindicates Jesus' claim

The resurrection proved that he was vindicated by God, and therefore the Messiah, the Son of God he claimed to be.

D. A. Carson

# VIDEO DISCUSSION #1: MAKING DEEPER CONNECTIONS TO THE BIBLE

1. Looking back at the Bible passage and your video teaching notes, what did you learn that you did not know previously? Consider specifically:

   • The significance of Jesus' statement about "sitting at the right hand of the Mighty One and coming on the clouds of heaven" in comparison to other Jewish literature about Metatron, David, etc.

   • The political charges that the Jewish leaders took to Pilate

   • The Jewish context of Jesus' claim to sit at the right hand of the Father

2. If you were Pilate or the high priest, do you think that you would have acted the same way that they did, or would you have acted differently?

3. Skim quickly through the biblical texts of the trial and crucifixion and list the many different titles given to Jesus (Son of Man, the King of the Jews, etc.).

4. Do you think Barabbas, the thief who was set free instead of Jesus, understood who Jesus was? Do you think he understood that he was released by Pilate while Jesus was sent to the cross? Do you think he realized that he was set free not only from physical death that day because of Jesus, but that Jesus' death also set him free spiritually?

# CONNECTING THE BIBLE TO LIFE

*You can have a restored relationship with the living God—not through what you do, but through what he did on the cross.*

## *Video Teaching #2 Notes*

Jesus is uniquely qualified to substitute for our sins

> For even the Son of Man did not come to be served, but to serve, and to give his life as a ransom for many.
>
> Mark 10:45

## Variety of reactions to Jesus on the cross

A large number of people followed him, including women who *mourned* and wailed for him.... The people stood watching, and the rulers even *sneered* at him.... The soldiers also came up and *mocked* him.... One of the criminals who hung there hurled *insults* at him.... But the other criminal rebuked him. "Don't you fear God," he said, "since you are under the same sentence?"... It was now about the sixth hour, and *darkness* came over the whole land until the ninth hour, for the sun stopped shining. And the *curtain* of the temple was torn in two.

Luke 23:27, 35–36, 39–40, 44–45

## The innocent Jesus dies for us

### DID YOU KNOW?

Darkness was associated in the ancient world with the death of great men.

David Garland

Crucifixion is one of the most abominable forms of torture and execution that the world has ever seen.

Robert Stein

With whom do you identify as you read about Jesus' death?

The resurrection vindicates
Jesus

What will we think of Jesus
when he looks us in the eye?

A restored relationship with God

I have come that they may have life, and have it to the full.

John 10:10

Jesus faces death so that others may have life.

Darrell Bock

The impact of Jesus' death

# VIDEO DISCUSSION #2: CONNECTING THE BIBLE TO LIFE

1. How would *you* reply to Darrell Bock's question, "Which group do you identify with as you read the story of Jesus' death? Do you sit and watch; do you mourn; do you defend Jesus like the thief on the cross?" Explain your answer.

2. Jesus suffered a cruel death on the cross and experienced separation from the Father ("My God, my God, why have you forsaken me?") when he felt the full weight of the world's sins. Do you agree with Darrell Bock when he says that one of the key questions that results from the trial and death of Jesus is whether or not we will let him take up *our* sins? If you have let him take your sins, can you remember how that felt?

3. Jesus left his home in heaven and was born in a humble stable. King Herod tried to kill him as a baby; he was rejected throughout his lifetime by the people he came to save/rescue; and he experienced intense suffering and death on a shameful cross. If you were Jesus, would you have done all that to save the world from their sins? Are you worth that much for Jesus to die for you? As a group, reflect on your worth to God and thank him for the great gift of his Son.

4. Darrell Bock says, "The good news of the gospel is that we can have a restored relationship with God — not through what *we* do, but through what *Jesus* did on the cross." Do you think that Christians need to *do* anything to receive salvation? If so, what?

# MAKING DEEPER CONNECTIONS IN YOUR OWN LIFE

*Personal reflection studies to do on your own*

## Day One

1. Read Matthew 26:57–27:55.

2. Isaac Watts wrote, "When I survey the wondrous cross on which the Prince of glory died; my richest gain I count but loss, and pour contempt on all my pride." What do these words mean to you? The last verse of that classic hymn concludes, "Love so amazing, so divine, demands my soul, my life, my all." Have you found that Jesus' sacrificial love demands *your* all? Does he have it?

3. If you were Jesus in the midst of an unfair trial, would you have been able to keep silent and not defend yourself? What about his rights? How does this apply in our relationships when others offend us? Are we quick to speak up and defend our rights? Is that okay to do?

# *Day Two*

1. Read Mark 14:43–15:41. Compare it with the Matthew account.

2. Jesus did not back down during his trial; in fact, he gave his accusers exactly the words they needed in order to send him to his death. The first Christians also faced suffering and persecution. In the modern Western world, our "persecution" is different, if there is any at all—and we can often avoid it by being silent about our beliefs and practices. Do you think that most North American believers try to blend in too much with the culture in order to be relevant, or at least not make waves? What about you? Do you avoid certain topics of conversation with friends and others to avoid trouble and possible rejection?

3. The soldiers played a game of "blind man's bluff" with Jesus after his arrest; to them, religion was a joke. We often see that same attitude in our culture, particularly in the arts and media. What could you do to help people see that Christianity is not a waste of time or a joke?

# Day Three

1. Read Luke 22:47–23:49. How does it differ from the Matthew and Mark accounts?

2. Throughout the trial and death of Jesus, the women remained faithful—they went to the cross and later to the tomb. But most of the apostles hid. How would you account for this? How does one remain faith-full in times of darkness, difficulty, and despair? What has helped you? Take your current struggles to the Lord in prayer right now; ask him to keep you faith-full.

3. Judas' betrayal made possible Jesus' trial and conviction. From a divine perspective, however, the cross was not a tragic mistake or a fatal flaw in God's plan. Jesus' prediction of his betrayal shows that the cross was what God intended all along. How do you think God's divine sovereignty and human responsibility play out in your life, and in the decisions that you make every single day?

# *Day Four*

1.  Read John 18:1–19:37, comparing it with the other three gospel accounts you've read.

2.  God is in control. In spite of all the disappointing and evil events surrounding Jesus' trial and death, the Son faithfully followed the Father and accomplished God's plan to rescue humanity, in fulfillment of Old Testament prophecies. Thank God for his master plan to save not only the world of its sins, but *yours*. Ask him what your role is in his ongoing plan. Record below any thoughts that he gives you.

3.  Darrell Bock talked about the Jewish disagreement over whether or not God shares his glory with others. Scripture is clear that God wants to be glorified in and through our lives. What does that look like for you? What do you do that really brings glory to God? Do you think he is happy with what he sees in your life?

# Day Five

1. Read Luke 22:66–23:3; 23:32–34, 44–47 one more time.

2. Pray through the entire passage verse by verse, allowing the deeper meaning that you have discovered to lead you as you pray. Ask the Spirit to continue to remind you of what you have learned and to help you apply these truths to your life. Jot down any further applications that come to mind as you pray.

3. Turn back to the discussion questions from the video teaching (Video Discussion #1, #2). If there are questions that your group did not have time to discuss or questions that you might like to think more about, use this time to review and reflect further.

## The Death of Death

# The Resurrection of Jesus (Matthew 28:1–10)

Dr. Gary Burge

Do not be afraid, for I know that you are looking for Jesus, who was crucified. He is not here; he has risen, just as he said.

*Matthew 28:5 – 6*

The sacrificial Lamb has become the risen Lord. That is the greatest truth mankind will ever know.

*Grant Osborne*

# INTRODUCTION

**Video Opener from Israel**

Garden Tomb

**Scripture Reading:** Matthew 28:1–10, followed by a prayer that God will open your heart as you study his Word

**Location of Passage:** Jerusalem; ancient tradition says that Jesus was buried in what is now the Church of the Holy Sepulchre, though others point to the Garden Tomb

Church of the Holy Sepulchre (c. 1870)

# MAKING DEEPER CONNECTIONS TO THE BIBLE

*The impossible has happened—the empty tomb and the appearances of Jesus change everything!*

## Video Teaching #1 Notes

**Location of Video Teaching:** Forest Home Cemetery, Chicago

The resurrection of Jesus: the center of the New Testament

## Peter's sermon

Men of Israel, listen to this: Jesus of Nazareth was a man accredited by God to you by miracles, wonders and signs, which God did among you through him, as you yourselves know. This man was handed over to you by God's set purpose and foreknowledge; and you, with the help of wicked men, put him to death by nailing him to the cross. But God raised him from the dead, freeing him from the agony of death, because it was impossible for death to keep its hold on him.

Acts 2:22–24

## Paul

If there is no resurrection of the dead, then not even Christ has been raised. And if Christ has not been raised, our preaching is useless and so is your faith.

1 Corinthians 15:13–14

## Jesus was crucified on a Friday afternoon

## The Sabbath (Saturday)

## Sunday morning ...

When the Sabbath was over, Mary Magdalene, Mary the mother of James, and Salome bought spices so that they might go to anoint Jesus' body. Very early on the first day of the week, just after sunrise, they were on their way to the tomb and they asked each other, "Who will roll the stone away from the entrance of the tomb?"

Mark 16:1 – 3

Given that the women had come to anoint a corpse, they did not expect a resurrection.

Darrell Bock

## The tomb was empty

Garden Tomb

> "Don't be alarmed," he said. "You are looking for Jesus the Nazarene, who was crucified. He has risen! He is not here. See the place where they laid him."
>
> Mark 16:6

The rolling away of the stone was not to let Jesus out, but to let the women in.

John Nolland

## The resurrection was unexpected

**DID YOU KNOW?**

The verb in "he is going ahead of you" is sometimes used of a commander making an advance or leading troops forward.

David Garland

## The women leave the tomb

> But go, tell his disciples and Peter, "He is going ahead of you into Galilee. There you will see him, just as he told you."
>
> Mark 16:7

## Peter and John run to the tomb

[John] saw and believed.

John 20:8

## Would the rest of the disciples believe?

"We are going up to Jerusalem," he said, "and the Son of Man will be betrayed to the chief priests and teachers of the law. They will condemn him to death and will hand him over to the Gentiles, who will mock him and spit on him, flog him and kill him. Three days later he will rise."

Mark 10:33–34

## Mary Magdalene

"Woman," he said, "why are you crying? Who is it you are looking for?" Thinking he was the gardener, she said, "Sir, if you have carried him away, tell me where you have put him, and I will get him."

John 20:15

## Jesus appears

Jesus said to her, "Mary." She turned toward him and cried out in Aramaic, "Rabboni!" (which means Teacher).

John 20:16

Jesus made a total of ten [post-resurrection] appearances.

Grant Osborne

Judaism had no ready-made doctrine of the resurrection

The Jewish authorities paid the guards to tell a lie

## DID YOU KNOW?

An early church leader, Chrysostom, remarked, "Jesus was buried with much myrrh, which glues linen to the body as firmly as lead."

Leon Morris

[John] bent over and looked in at the strips of linen lying there but did not go in. Then Simon Peter, who was behind him, arrived and went into the tomb. He saw the strips of linen lying there, as well as the burial cloth that had been around Jesus' head. The cloth was folded up by itself, separate from the linen.

John 20:5–7

Women as witnesses to the resurrection

The tomb of Jesus never became a shrine

The early Christians talk about the resurrection

But God raised him from the dead, freeing him from the agony of death, because it was impossible for death to keep its hold on him.

Acts 2:24

Too many people attend Easter services and then go back to their lives as normal. They are neither filled with awe, nor impelled to tell anyone about the story. What stops it from being told?

David Garland

# VIDEO DISCUSSION #1: MAKING DEEPER CONNECTIONS TO THE BIBLE

1. Looking back at the Bible passage and your video teaching notes, what did you learn that you did not know previously? Consider specifically:

   • The centrality of the resurrection in early Christian sermons

   *God*      *Father*
   *Jesus*      *Son*
   *Holy Spirit*      *Spirit*

   • The details of what happened to Jesus' body after his death

   • The fact that Judaism did not expect a resurrection of a single individual within time

   • The various arguments for the historicity of the resurrection

2. Gary Burge said that the resurrection was the main theme of early Christian preaching. Why do you think the resurrection is so important? Is it important in *your* life? Why or why not?

3. Gary Burge concluded this section by stating that when people see spectacular things, they talk about them. He then mentioned that the first Christians who saw the resurrected Jesus spoke about him with boldness and confidence. Do you think that Christians today have "seen" the spectacular nature of Jesus' resurrection? Do you think that Christians today talk about the resurrection with boldness and confidence? What about you?

4. One of the key evidences for the resurrection is the fact that no Jew living in the first century expected someone to be resurrected from the dead until the end of the world. Thus, when other "messianic" figures in the first century, such as Bar Kochba, died, their followers did not solve the problem of their disappointing deaths by inventing stories of their resurrection. Why do you think the disciples of Jesus spread the message of the resurrection? Does it make any sense to invent such a story if it were not true? How could this information be helpful as you talk with non-Christians about the resurrection?

# CONNECTING THE BIBLE TO LIFE

*As death did not defeat Christ, death will not defeat Christ's people.*

## *Video Teaching #2 Notes*

The Good Shepherd

> I am the good shepherd; I know my sheep and my sheep know me — just as the Father knows me and I know the Father — and I lay down my life for the sheep.... No one takes it from me, but I lay it down of my own accord.
>
> John 10:14 – 15, 18

The death of Jesus is a work for us, but so is the resurrection

How is the resurrection vital for our faith?

The resurrection is at the heart of primitive Christian hope.

Darrell Bock

The resurrection is the historical anchor that validates Jesus' teachings

> Therefore go and make disciples of all nations, baptizing them in the name of the Father and of the Son and of the Holy Spirit, and teaching them to obey everything I have commanded you.
>
> Matthew 28:19–20

If I were Peter, beating myself with guilt in some grubby hiding place, and then were to hear that the risen Lord has invited me by name to meet with him as he had promised, I would know that he still loved me and would break every record to get to his side.

David McKenna

The resurrection means Jesus is living today

## The resurrection defeats death

> The tombs broke open and the bodies of many holy people who had died were raised to life.
>
> Matthew 27:52
>
> ———————————— ◎ ————————————
>
> Where, O death, is your victory? Where, O death, is your sting?
>
> 1 Corinthians 15:55

## We are united to Jesus in his resurrection

## Jesus defeated death and ascended as a *human*

> For we do not have a high priest who is unable to sympathize with our weaknesses, but we have one who has been tempted in every way, just as we are — yet was without sin.
>
> Hebrews 4:15

The one who has risen is the same Jesus who was crucified.

R. T. France

## The saving work of Christ is found in the cross *and* in the resurrection

> I want to know Christ and the power of his resurrection and the fellowship of sharing in his sufferings, becoming like him in his death, and so, somehow, to attain to the resurrection from the dead.
>
> Philippians 3:10–11

Story of Barbara

Confidence in our own resurrection

> I am the resurrection and the life. He who believes in me will live, even though he dies; and whoever lives and believes in me will never die.
>
> John 11:25–26

# VIDEO DISCUSSION #2: CONNECTING THE BIBLE TO LIFE

1. Gary Burge started this section by stating that a good shepherd protects his sheep by placing himself between them and danger. How does it make you feel that the Good Shepherd who protects you is the resurrected, all-powerful Lord? Given that he cares for us, do you think that he is protecting us on a daily basis? How have you seen this in your life?

2.  In the resurrection, God put his stamp of approval upon Jesus' life and teachings. Do you think that Jesus' teachings play a central role in Christian ethics today? In other words, do you think that we Christians try to model our lives upon what Jesus did and taught? The pat answer is to say yes, but do you think that is really true? Why or why not?

3.  Describe an experience that you had at a funeral where it really made a difference that Jesus defeated death.

4.  How does the fact that Jesus defeated death affect your own life since you know that some day you also will face death? Do you have confidence in your own resurrection to life? Why or why not?

# MAKING DEEPER CONNECTIONS IN YOUR OWN LIFE

*Personal reflection studies to do on your own*

## Day One

1. Read Matthew 28:1–15.

2. The resurrection of Jesus Christ changes everything. Because he lives and offers forgiveness, we can have a new relationship with God through him. Do you often reflect on the fact that Jesus is now alive through the resurrection, and that he desires regular fellowship with you? Do you spend much time with him? Why or why not?

3. David Garland says, "Too many people attend Easter services and then go back to their lives as normal. They are neither filled with awe, nor impelled to tell anyone about the story." What about you? How has the resurrection story impacted your life? Has it impelled you to tell the story to others? With whom could you share the story?

# Day Two

1. Read Mark 16:1–8. Compare it with Matthew's version of the resurrection.

2. The resurrection shows us that death is not the end. Like Jesus, we who have trusted him as our Savior will be resurrected to eternal life with God in heaven. What do you think heaven will be like? Who/what do you *most* look forward to seeing/doing there? What do you *least* look forward to?

3. The fact that we will be resurrected also means that we will be held accountable to God for what we do in *this* life. There will be no reruns, no do-overs. Do you look forward to meeting the "Judge"? Why or why not? Do you think there will be more or less grace than you deserve? What do you least look forward to talking to the Lord about on that day? (See pastor and author Pete Briscoe's dramatic, one-man account of what it will be like when we meet Jesus: "The Bema: Judgment Seat of Christ" at https://www.tellingthetruth.org/catalog/netProduct. aspx?ilD=16343.)

# Day Three

1. Read Luke 24. Compare Luke's version of the resurrection to those of Matthew and Mark.

2. N. T. Wright and others have shown that Judaism did not possess a ready-made doctrine of the resurrection for the disciples to "borrow." Why do you think this fact is important in our argument for the truthfulness/credibility of the resurrection?

3. Review the arguments presented throughout Gary Burge's study to defend the empty tomb and show that the story of the resurrection is plausible and believable. Can you think of additional arguments? For a more challenging project, check out some of the best books on the historicity of the resurrection by such authors as Lee Strobel, Gary Habermas, William Craig, or N. T. Wright.

# *Day Four*

1. Read John 20, then compare it with the other three gospel accounts of the resurrection.

2. Now that you have read all of the gospel accounts of the resurrection, go back and note the various portions that show skepticism about it. Why do you think the people were skeptical? How does Scripture answer their skepticism? The typical apologetical arguments for the resurrection might convince some skeptics, but no one can argue with a changed life. What parts of your faith story could you tell a skeptical friend? Jot down the highlights of your story and practice telling it so that you are ready when the opportunity arises.

3. We are impacted by Jesus' death, but also by his resurrection. Paul argues in Romans 6:1–14 that it is Jesus' resurrection that motivates us to overcome sin in our lives. Read and meditate on this passage, pondering how your life is going in terms of Paul's words.

# Day Five

1. Read Matthew 28:1–10 one more time.

2. Pray through the entire passage verse by verse, allowing the deeper meaning that you have discovered to lead you as you pray. Ask the Spirit to continue to remind you of what you have learned and to help you apply these truths to your life. Jot down any further applications that come to mind as you pray.

3. Turn back to the discussion questions from the video teaching (Video Discussion #1, #2). If there are questions that your group did not have time to discuss or questions that you might like to think more about, use this time to review and reflect further.

# Source Acknowledgments

*(These are noted in order of appearance for each session. Full source information can be found in "Books for Further Reading" beginning on page 133.)*

## Session 1

Page 11: Bock, *Jesus According to Scripture*, 233.
Page 16: Blomberg, *Jesus and the Gospels*, 279.
Page 16: Carson, *Matthew*, 633.
Page 17: Hurtado, *Mark*, 141.
Page 18: Walker, *Steps of Jesus*, 94.
Page 20: Ibid.
Page 24: Ibid., 206.
Page 25: France, *Matthew*, 638.
Page 25: Garland, *Mark*, 338.

## Session 2

Page 33: France, *Matthew*, 644.
Page 35: Moo, *2 Peter*, 72–73.
Page 36: Bock, *Luke*, NIVAC, 272.
Page 37: Davies, *Matthew*, 703.
Page 38: *IVP Women's Bible Commentary*, 528.
Page 38: Walker, *Steps of Jesus*, 95.
Page 40: Garland, *Mark*, 352.
Page 42: Hagner, *Matthew*, 495.
Page 44: Nolland, *Matthew*, 704.
Page 45: France, *Matthew*, 647.
Page 45: Garland, *Mark*, 348.

## Session 3

Page 53: Garland, *Mark*, 430.
Page 54: Turner, *Matthew*, 496.
Page 55: Walker, *Steps of Jesus*, 116.
Page 56: Garland, *Mark*, 429.
Page 57: Bock, *Luke*, NIVAC, 497.
Page 58: France, *Matthew*, 770.
Page 60: Bock, *Luke*, 1559.
Page 61: Bock, *Jesus According to Scripture*, 315.

## Session 4

Page 69: Strauss, *Luke*, 166.
Page 71: Osborne, *John*, 197.
Page 73: *IVP Women's Bible Commentary*, 539.
Page 74: Strauss, *Luke*, 166.
Page 75: Evans, *Bible Knowledge Background Commentary*, 476–477.
Page 76: Walker, *Steps of Jesus*, 123.
Page 77: Bock, *Luke*, NIVAC, 551.
Page 78: Morris, *Matthew*, 544.
Page 80: Wilkins, *Matthew*, NIVAC, 838.

## Session 5

Page 87: Walker, *Steps of Jesus*, 203.
Page 89: Ibid., 177.
Page 89: Garland, *Mark*, 571.
Page 90: Ibid., 90.
Page 93: Ibid., 92.
Page 95: Carson, *John*, 632.
Page 98: Garland, *Mark*, 99.
Page 98: Stein, *Jesus the Messiah*, 245.
Page 99: Bock, *Luke*, NIVAC, 579.

## Session 6

Page 107: Osborne, *John*, 290.
Page 110: Garland, *Mark*, 105.
Page 110: Bock, *Luke*, 1895.
Page 111: Nolland, *Matthew*, 1250.
Page 111: Garland, *Mark*, 614.
Page 113: Osborne, *John*, 284.

Page 114: Morris, *Matthew*, 735.
Page 115: Garland, *Mark*, 629.
Page 118: Bock, *Luke*, 1883.
Page 119: McKenna, *Mark*, 325.
Page 121: France, *Matthew*, 407.

# Map and Photo Credits

# Books for Further Reading

## Life of Jesus

Bailey, Kenneth E. *Jesus Through Middle Eastern Eyes: Cultural Studies in the Gospels.* Downers Grove, Ill.: InterVarsity, 2008.

Blomberg, Craig L. *Jesus and the Gospels: An Introduction and Survey.* Nashville: Broadman and Holman, 1997.

Bock, Darrell L. *Jesus According to Scripture: Restoring the Portrait from the Gospels.* Grand Rapids, Mich.: Baker, 2002.

Stein, Robert H. *Jesus the Messiah: A Survey of the Life of Christ.* Downers Grove, Ill.: InterVarsity, 1996.

Strauss, Mark L. *Four Portraits, One Jesus: An Introduction to Jesus and the Gospels.* Grand Rapids, Mich.: Zondervan, 2007.

Walker, Peter. *In the Steps of Jesus: An Illustrated Guide to the Places of the Holy Land.* Grand Rapids, Mich.: Zondervan, 2006.

## Four Gospels

Beale, G. K. and D. A. Carson. *Commentary on the New Testament Use of the Old Testament.* Grand Rapids, Mich.: Baker, 2007.

Evans, Craig A., gen. ed. *The Bible Knowledge Background Commentary: Matthew–Luke.* Colorado Springs: Victor Books, 2003.

Keener, Craig S. *The IVP Bible Background Commentary: New Testament.* Downers Grove, Ill.: InterVarsity Press, 1993.

Kroeger, Catherine Clark and Mary J. Evans, eds. *The IVP Women's Bible Commentary.* Downers Grove, Ill.: InterVarsity Press, 2002.

## Matthew

Barton, Bruce B. *Matthew.* Life Application Bible Commentary. Wheaton, Ill.: Tyndale, 1996.

Blomberg, Craig L. *Matthew*. New American Commentary, vol. 22. Nashville, Tenn.: Broadman Press, 1992.

Carson, D. A. *Matthew, Mark, Luke*. The Expositor's Bible Commentary, vol. 8. Grand Rapids, Mich.: Zondervan, 1984.

Davies, W. D., Dale C. Allison Jr. *A Critical and Exegetical Commentary on the Gospel According to Saint Matthew*. The International Critical Commentary. 3 vols. Edinburgh: T&T Clark, 1988, 1991, 1997.

France, R. T. *The Gospel According to Matthew: An Introduction and Commentary*. Tyndale New Testament Commentaries, vol. 1. Grand Rapids, Mich.: Eerdmans, 1985.

France, R. T. *The Gospel of Matthew*. The New International Commentary on the New Testament. Grand Rapids, Mich.: Eerdmans, 2007.

Green, Michael. *The Message of Matthew: The Kingdom of Heaven*. The Bible Speaks Today Series. Downers Grove, Ill.: InterVarsity Press, 2000.

Guelich, Robert A. *Sermon on the Mount: A Foundation for Understanding*. Waco, Tex.: Word, 1982.

Gundry, Robert. *Matthew: A Commentary on His Handbook for a Mixed Church Under Persecution*. Grand Rapids, Mich.: Eerdmans, 2nd ed., 1994.

Hagner, Donald. *Matthew*. Word Biblical Commentary, vol. 33 a&b. Waco, Tex.: Word, 1993, 1995.

Keener, Craig S. *A Commentary on the Gospel of Matthew*. Grand Rapids, Mich.: Eerdmans, 1999.

Morris, Leon. *The Gospel According to Matthew*. The Pillar New Testament Commentary. Grand Rapids, Mich.: Eerdmans, 1992.

Mounce, Robert H. *Matthew*. New International Biblical Commentary, vol. 1. Peabody, Mass.: Hendrickson, 1991.

Nolland, John. *The Gospel of Matthew: A Commentary on the Greek Text*. The New International Greek Testament Commentary. Grand Rapids, Mich.: Eerdmans, 2005.

Simonetti, Manlio, ed. *Matthew*. Ancient Christian Commentary on Scripture. 2 vols. Downers Grove, Ill.: InterVarsity Press, 2002.

Turner, David L. *Matthew*. Baker Exegetical Commentary on the New Testament. Grand Rapids, Mich.: Baker, 2008.

Turner, David L. and Darrell L. Bock. *The Gospel of Matthew/The Gospel of Mark*. Cornerstone Biblical Commentary. Wheaton, Ill.: Tyndale, 2006.

Wilkins, Michael J. *Matthew: From Biblical Text to Contemporary Life*. The NIV Application Commentary. Grand Rapids, Mich.: Zondervan, 2004.

_____. Zondervan Illustrated Bible Backgrounds Commentary. Grand Rapids, Mich.: Zondervan, 2002.

# Mark

Cole, R. Alan. *The Gospel According to Mark.* Tyndale New Testament Commentaries, vol. 2. Grand Rapids, Mich.: Eerdmans, 2002.

Cranfield, C. E. B. *The Gospel According to Saint Mark: An Introduction and Commentary.* Cambridge Greek Testament Commentary. Cambridge University Press, 1972.

Edwards, James R. *The Gospel According to Mark.* The Pillar New Testament Commentary. Grand Rapids, Mich.: Eerdmans, 2002.

Evans, Craig. *Mark.* Word Biblical Commentary, vol. 34b. Nashville: Thomas Nelson, 2001.

Fackler, Mark. *Mark.* Life Application Bible Commentary. Wheaton, Ill.: Tyndale, 1994.

France, R. T. *The Gospel of Mark: A Commentary on the Greek Text.* The New International Greek New Testament Commentary. Grand Rapids, Mich.: Eerdmans, 2002.

Garland, David E. *Mark.* The NIV Application Commentary. Grand Rapids, Mich.: Zondervan, 1996.

———. *Mark.* Zondervan Illustrated Bible Backgrounds Commentary. Grand Rapids, Mich.: Zondervan, 2002.

Guelich, Robert A. *Mark.* Word Biblical Commentary, vol. 34a. Dallas, Tex.: Word, 1989.

Gundry, Robert H. *A Commentary on His Apology for the Cross.* Grand Rapids, Mich.: Eerdmans, 1993.

Hurtado, Larry. *Mark.* New International Biblical Commentary. Peabody, Mass.: Hendrickson, 1995.

Lane, William L. *The Gospel According to Mark: The English Text with Introduction, Exposition, and Notes.* The New International Commentary on the New Testament. Grand Rapids, Mich.: Eerdmans, 1974.

McKenna, David L. *Mark.* The Communicator's Commentary Series, vol. 2. Dallas: Word, 1982.

Oden, Thomas C. and Christopher A. Hall, eds. *Mark.* Ancient Christian Commentary on Scripture, vol. 2. Downers Grove, Ill.: InterVarsity Press, 1998.

Stein, Robert H. *Mark.* Baker Exegetical Commentary on the New Testament. Grand Rapids, Mich.: Baker, 2008.

Taylor, Vincent. *The Gospel According to St. Mark: The Greek Text with Introduction, Notes, and Indexes.* Thornapple Commentaries. Grand Rapids, Mich.: Baker, 2nd ed., 1981.

Wessel, Walter W. *Matthew, Mark, Luke.* The Expositor's Bible Commentary, vol. 8. Grand Rapids, Mich.: Zondervan, 1984.

Witherington, Ben III. *The Gospel of Mark: A Socio-Rhetorical Commentary.* Grand Rapids, Mich.: Eerdmans, 2001.

## Luke

Barton, Bruce B., Dave Veerman, and Linda K. Taylor. *Luke.* Life Application Bible Commentary. Wheaton, Ill.: Tyndale, 1997.

Bock, Darrell L. *Luke.* The NIV Application Commentary Series. Grand Rapids, Mich.: Zondervan, 1996.

Bock, Darrell L. *Luke 1:1:1–9:50; 9:51–24:53.* Baker Exegetical Commentary on the New Testament, 2 vols. Grand Rapids, Mich.: Baker, 1996.

Evans, Craig A. *Luke.* New International Biblical Commentary, vol. 3. Peabody, Mass.: Hendrickson, 1990.

Fitzmyer, J. A. *The Gospel According to Luke: Introduction, Translation, and Notes.* Anchor Bible, vol. 28–28a. Garden City, N.Y.: Doubleday, 1981–1985.

Green, Joel B. *The Gospel of Luke.* New International Commentary on the New Testament. Grand Rapids, Mich.: Eerdmans, 1997.

Just, Arther A. Jr., ed. *Luke.* Ancient Christian Commentary on Scripture, vol. 3. Downers Grove, Ill.: InterVarsity Press, 2003.

Larson, Bruce. *Luke.* The Preacher's Commentary, vol. 26. Nashville: Thomas Nelson, 1983.

Liefeld, Walter L. *Matthew, Mark, Luke.* The Expositor's Bible Commentary, vol. 8. Grand Rapids, Mich.: Zondervan, 1984.

Marshall, I. Howard. *Luke: Historian and Theologian.* Grand Rapids, Mich.: Zondervan, 1980.

Morris, Leon. *Luke, An Introduction and Commentary.* Tyndale New Testament Commentaries, vol. 3. Grand Rapids, Mich.: Eerdmans, 1988.

Nolland, John. *Luke.* Word Biblical Commentary, vol. 35a–c. Dallas: Word, 1989–1993.

Stein, Robert H. *Luke.* The New American Commentary, vol. 24. Nashville: Broadman, 1992.

Strauss, Mark L. *Luke.* Zondervan Illustrated Bible Backgrounds Commentary. Grand Rapids, Mich.: Zondervan, 2002.

## John

Barrett, C. K. *The Gospel According to St. John: An Introduction with Commentary and Notes on the Greek Text.* Philadelphia: Westminster Press, 1978.

Barton, Bruce B. *John.* Life Application Bible Commentary. Wheaton, Ill.: Tyndale, 1993.

Beasley-Murray, George R. *John.* Word Biblical Commentaries, vol. 36. Nashville: Thomas Nelson, 1999.

Brown, Raymond Edward. *The Gospel According to John.* Anchor Bible, vol. 29–29a. Garden City, N.Y., Doubleday, 1966–1970.

Burge, Gary M. *John.* The NIV Application Commentary. Grand Rapids, Mich.: Zondervan, 2000.

Card, Michael. *The Parable of Joy: Reflections on the Wisdom of the Book of John.* Nashville: Thomas Nelson, 1995.

Carson, Donald A. *The Gospel According to John.* The Pillar New Testament Commentary. Grand Rapids, Mich.:Eerdmans, 1991.

Keener, Craig S. *The Gospel of John : A Commentary.* 2 vols. Peabody, Mass.: Hendrickson, 2003.

Köstenberger, Andreas J. *John.* Baker Exegetical Commentary on the New Testament. Grand Rapids, Mich.: Baker, 2004.

———. *John.* Zondervan Illustrated Bible Backgrounds Commentary. Grand Rapids, Mich.: Zondervan, 2002.

Morris, Leon. *The Gospel According to John.* New International Commentary on the New Testament. Grand Rapids, Mich.: Eerdmans, 1995.

Osborne, Grant R. *The Gospel of John.* Cornerstone Biblical Commentary, vol. 13. Carol Stream, IL: Tyndale, 2007.

Tasker, R. V. G. *The Gospel According to St. John : An Introduction and Commentary.* Tyndale New Testament Commentaries. Grand Rapids, Mich.: Eerdmans, 1960.

Tenney, Merrill C. *John, Acts.* The Expositor's Bible Commentary, vol. 9. Grand Rapids, Mich.: Zondervan, 1984.

Whitacre, Rodney A. *John.* The IVP New Testament Commentary Series, vol. 4. Downers Grove, Ill.: InterVarsity Press, 1999.

# The Miracles of Jesus

## Six In-depth Studies
## Connecting the Bible to Life

*Matt Williams, General Editor*

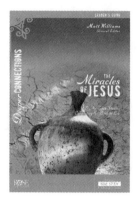

Healer of diseases. Master of nature. Conqueror of demons and death. Jesus not only preached the kingdom of God in word, but he demonstrated it in power through his miraculous deeds. In six engaging, interactive small group sessions, this Deeper Connections DVD study gives you a unique, in-depth look at the miracles of Jesus and will open your eyes to their impact on the lives he touched, what they reveal about God's heart, and their significance for us today.

The six sessions are:

- The Clean Daughter (Mark 5:21–34)
- The Heartbeat of God (John 2:1–11)
- Knowing the King (Matt. 14:15–33)
- A Faith-full Outsider (Matt. 15:21–28)
- Fruitless Lives (Mark 11:12–21)
- Grateful Outcasts (Luke 17:11–19)

Taught and written by Bible professors, this DVD study with participant's guide explores the historical background of the Bible, its text, and its application for your life today. Filmed on location in the US and Israel, the Deeper Connections series is designed for small groups and Bible study classes.

DVD: 9781628624304
Participant's Guide: 9781628624311

*Pick up a copy today at your favorite bookstore!*

# CHRISTIAN HISTORY MADE EASY

12-Session DVD Study for Individual or Group Use
by Timothy Paul Jones, PhD

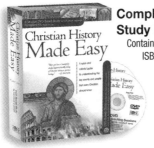

### Complete *Christian History Made Easy* Study Kit
Contains each of the following items
ISBN: 9781596365254

### The DVD
• All 12 DVD sessions, each about 30 minutes • Leader Guide on disc as a printable PDF • Fliers, bulletin inserts, posters & banners as PDFs on disc.
ISBN: 9781596365261

### Leader Guide
• Leader Guide gives step-by-step instructions for group hosts or facilitators so you don't have to be the expert.
ISBN: 9781596365278

### Participant Guide
• Purchase one for each participant.
• Includes group discussion questions, session outlines, key terms and definitions, Bible study questions, and more.
ISBN: 9781596365285

### PowerPoint® Presentation
• Contains more than 300 slides to expand the scope of the teaching  ISBN: 9781596363410

### *Christian History Made Easy* Book
• 224 pages, paperback
ISBN: 9781596363281

# HOW WE GOT THE BIBLE

## DVD Bible Study for Individual or Group Use

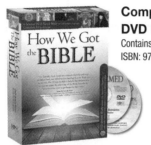

### Complete *How We Got the Bible* DVD Bible Study Kit

Contains each of the following items
ISBN: 9781628622072

### *How We Got the Bible* DVD Bible Study

• All six DVD sessions • Leader Guide on disc as a printable PDF •
Fliers, bulletin inserts, posters & banners as PDFs on disc
ISBN: 9781628622065

### Leader Guide

• Leader Guide gives step-by-step instructions for group hosts or facilitators so you don't have to be the expert.
ISBN: 9781628622089

### Participant Guide

• Purchase one for each participant.
• Includes group discussion questions, session outlines, key terms and definitions, Bible study questions, and more.
ISBN: 9781628622126

### PowerPoint® presentation

• Contains more than 100 slides to expand the scope of the teaching  ISBN: 9781890947460

### Pamphlet

• Fold-out time line of key events
ISBN: 9781628620825

### *How We Got the Bible* handbook

• Goes into more depth
• Explores the historical background
• 180-page paperback
ISBN: 9781628622164

# FEASTS OF THE BIBLE

## DVD Bible Study for Individual or Group Use

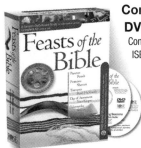

### Complete *Feasts of the Bible* DVD Bible Study Kit

Contains each of the following items
ISBN: 9781596364646

### *Feasts of the Bible* DVD Bible Study

• All six DVD-based sessions •
Leader Guide on disc as a printable PDF • Fliers,
bulletin inserts, posters & banners as PDFs on disc
ISBN: 9781596364653

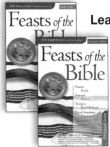

### Leader Guide

• Leader Guide gives step-by-step instructions for group
hosts or facilitators so you don't have to be the expert
ISBN: 9781596364660

### Participant Guide

• Each participant will need a guide
• Guide contains definitions, charts, comparisons,
Bible references, discussion questions, and more
ISBN: 9781596364677

### *Feasts of the Bible* PowerPoint® presentation

• Contains more than 100 slides to expand the scope
of the teaching  ISBN: 9781596361775

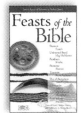

### *Feasts of the Bible* pamphlet

• Chart showing each feast, the date, biblical passage, and
symbolism fulfilled by Jesus
ISBN: 9781890947583

### Messiah in the Feasts of Israel handbook

• Goes into greater depth on all the feasts
• Gives insights into God's redemptive plan, discusses
the prophetic purposes of the feasts
• 236-page paperback
ISBN: 9780970261977

We want to hear from you. Please send your comments about this book to us in care of info@hendricksonrose.com. Thank you.

www.hendricksonrose.com